Trout

Purchased with funds from the
Library Services & Technology Act
Youth Materials Grant

Trout

by Cherie Winner

A Carolrhoda Nature Watch Book

Carolrhoda Books, Inc. / Minneapolis

For my parents, Vernon and Helen Olsen

The author thanks the following for sharing their knowledge of the complex world of trout: Dr. Robert Behnke and Dr. Kurt Fausch, Department of Fishery and Wildlife Biology, Colorado State University; Dr. Theodore Bjornn, Department of Fish and Wildlife Resources, University of Idaho–Moscow; Dr. Roy Stein, Department of Zoology, Ohio State University; and Dr. Robert Butler, Department of Biology, Pennsylvania State University.

Carolrhoda Books, Inc., c/o The Lerner Publishing Group
241 First Avenue North, Minneapolis, MN 55401 U.S.A.

Website address: www.lernerbooks.com

LIBRARY OF CONGRESS CATALOGING-IN-PUBLICATION DATA

Winner, Cherie.
  Trout / by Cherie Winner.
    p. cm.
  "A Carolrhoda nature watch book."
  Includes index.
  Summary: Describes the physical characteristics, life cycle, and habitat of trout, as well as threats to their existence.
  ISBN 1-57505-245-8
  1. Trout—Juvenile literature. [1. Trout.] I. Title.
QL638.S2W57   1998
597.5′7—dc21   97-15497

Manufactured in the United States of America
1 2 3 4 5 6 – JR – 03 02 01 00 99 98

Photographs are reproduced through the courtesy of: © Gustav W. Verderber/Visuals Unlimited, front cover, p. 27; © Bernd Wittich/Visuals Unlimited, back cover, p. 9 (bottom); © Breck P. Kent, pp. 2, 28 (bottom), 33 (bottom), 34 (top right, bottom), 35, 36 (top), 44; © Peter Ziminski/Visuals Unlimited, pp. 5, 8 (bottom); © Dale C. Spartas/THE GREEN AGENCY, p. 6; © Mack Henley/Visuals Unlimited, p. 8 (top); © Ken Lucas/Visuals Unlimited, p. 9 (top); © Jim Yuskavitch, pp. 10 (bottom), 11 (right), 20, 29 (both), 32, 38 (both), 40 (right), 41 (left); © Robert E. Barber, pp. 10 (top left), 31 (left); © LuRay Parker, Wyoming Game and Fish Department, pp. 10 (top right), 43; © Richard T. Grost, pp. 11 (left), 19 (both), 21, 22, 23, 24, 25, 31 (right), 33 (top), 34 (top left), 36 (bottom), 37 (both), 39 (bottom right), 45; © Bill Buckley/THE GREEN AGENCY, pp. 12 (both), 16, 17; © Bill Kamin/Visuals Unlimited, p. 14; Steven Campana, Bedford Institute, p. 15; © John G. Shedd Aquarium, pp. 18, 30; © Walt Anderson/Visuals Unlimited, p. 26; © Joe McDonald/Visuals Unlimited, p. 28 (top); Minnesota Water and Pollution Control Agency/IPS, p. 39 (bottom left); © Link/Visuals Unlimited, p. 39 (top); © Dr. John Rinne, p. 40 (left); © Ron Goede, Utah Division of Wildlife Resources, p. 41 (right); © Tim Peterson/Visuals Unlimited, p. 42. Map on p. 7 by Michael Tacheny, copyright © 1998 Carolrhoda Books, Inc. Illustration on p. 13 by John Erste, copyright © 1998 Carolrhoda Books, Inc.

CONTENTS

THE REMARKABLE TROUT

On a hot summer afternoon, a plump grasshopper tries to jump across a stream. It misses and tumbles into the water. Below, a lurking trout sees the grasshopper struggle to jump back into the air. Swiftly the trout rises. It opens its mouth wide, and the grasshopper disappears in a swirl of water. The trout returns to its cool hiding place to watch for another bite of food to come its way.

For centuries, humans have marveled at the grace, beauty, and strength of trout. We have written stories about them, painted pictures of them, and relished eating them. Fishers flock to the wilderness areas where trout live, hoping to catch just a few of these remarkable fish.

There are about 10 **species**, or kinds, of trout. The name *trout* comes from *trōktēs*, a Greek word meaning "one who gnaws." Trout belong to the family Salmonidae (sal-MON-ih-dee), which also includes the fish called salmon and char. In some cases, people have confused the names trout and char. For example, brook trout *(Salvelinus fontinalis)* should really be called char. But people have called them trout for many years because they're very similar to trout. This book talks about all fish that are commonly called trout.

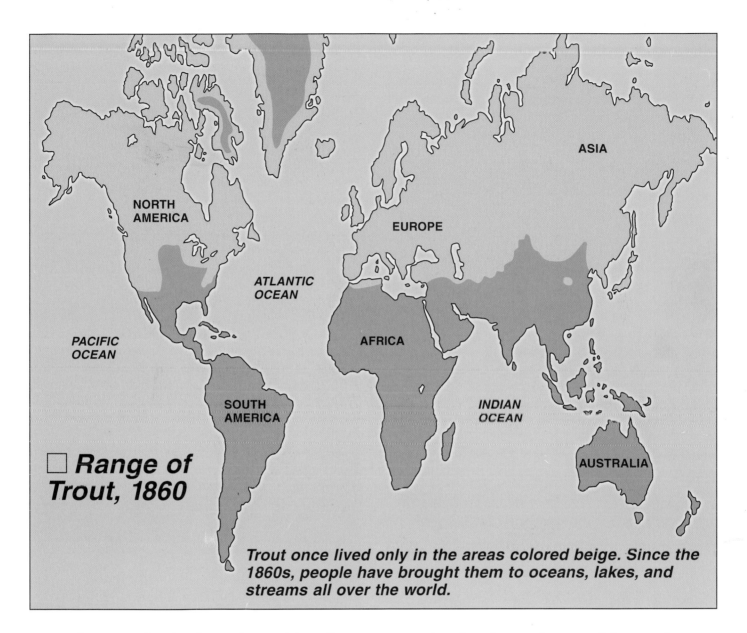

Range of Trout, 1860

Trout once lived only in the areas colored beige. Since the 1860s, people have brought them to oceans, lakes, and streams all over the world.

Biologists think the Salmonidae first appeared about one hundred million years ago, making them one of the oldest families of fish in the world. They originally lived only in the Northern Hemisphere. Their **range**, or area where they live, has expanded to include Australia, New Zealand, southern Africa, and parts of South America as well. Trout first reached these new homes in the 1860s, when fishers started taking them from Europe and North America to lakes and streams in the Southern Hemisphere.

Trout can thrive in huge lakes (above) *and in small streams* (right).

Trout live in many different **habitats**, or kinds of environments, throughout their range. They live in small creeks, large rivers, and lakes. Many trout spend part of their lives in freshwater and part in the salty ocean.

Despite these differences, trout have several things in common. They all breed and grow up in freshwater. Almost all trout move, or **migrate**, from one area to another at different times in their lives. And they all need to live in cool, very clean water.

A COLORFUL FAMILY

Trout are known for another trait they share: their extraordinary colors. Trout are among the most beautiful fish in the world. They may be bright green or gold. Many have rosy cheeks and sides. Almost all trout glisten with black, red, or blue spots.

Even the lake trout *(Salvelinus namaycush)*, which looks drab compared to many other trout, is a shiny silvery-blue. Some lake trout have orange-red fins. Lake trout also have light spots and squiggles on their backs and sides.

Rainbow trout *(Oncorhynchus mykiss)* got their name from the rosy, rainbow-like bands along their sides. Many have rosy cheeks, and all have black spots.

Left: *Lake trout look duller than other kinds of trout, but they have beautiful patterns.*
Top: *A bright rainbow trout*

Above left: *A cutthroat trout*
Above: *A brook trout*

There are many kinds of cutthroat trout (*Oncorhynchus clarki*). Some are silver all over with a rosy tinge. Others are gold, orange, or greenish. All have dark spots. Some cutthroats have just a few large splotches, while others have hundreds of tiny spots that look like sprinkles of pepper. The cutthroat's name comes from the slash of bright red or orange under its jaw, which makes it look as if its throat has been cut.

Brook trout have olive green sides speckled with gold spots and squiggles, and a few red spots surrounded by light blue halos.

Most brown trout *(Salmo trutta)* aren't actually brown—they're dark gold or olive green. They have big red and black spots surrounded by light rings. Some brown trout are silver with black spots.

Above: *A brown trout*

These five species—lake trout, rainbow trout, cutthroat trout, brook trout, and brown trout—are the best-known trout in North America. Their colors may change depending on season, temperature, and habitat. Some trout live their whole lives in freshwater, while others live in salt water part of the time. When trout move between freshwater and salt water, they change color. For example, rainbow trout that migrate to the ocean become silvery-blue. For this reason, they are known as steelheads.

Steelheads aren't silver all the time, though. Like all trout, steelheads undergo spectacular changes in color as they prepare to mate. Their bodies produce chemicals called **hormones**, which travel through the blood and make the males turn orange, pink, or red along their sides and belly. The orange marks on the throats of male cutthroat trout become bigger and brighter than usual. These brighter colors probably help males attract mates. Females may also become more brightly colored at mating time, but they usually do not change as much as the males do.

A steelhead is a shiny silver color (above) *until it's time to mate* (left).

LIVING UNDERWATER

Although trout are famous for their beautiful colors, they're much more than just pretty animals. Like all fish, trout have complex **adaptations**, or special features, that help the trout to do underwater many of the things humans do on land. Trout must get oxygen, find food, sense danger, protect their bodies from injury and infection, and find their way on long journeys—all underwater.

The trout's skin has adapted to protect the trout and help it move quickly underwater. The skin contains thousands of hard, clear, oval disks called **scales**. Each scale overlaps the scale behind it.

Scales help shield the trout from rocks and sticks it might bump against in the water. If a trout suffers a cut or scrape, the wound could become infected and the trout could die.

In the trout's skin, beneath its scales, lie the pigments, or colors, that make the trout so beautiful. The skin also contains cells that produce a slimy layer of **mucus** that covers the trout's whole body. Trout are among the most slippery fish on Earth. Mucus helps trout zip through the water. The layer of slime also helps repel bacteria that cause dangerous infections and diseases.

Above: *Scales provide underwater armor for a rainbow trout.*
Left: *This cutthroat trout looks slimy because it's covered by a layer of mucus.*

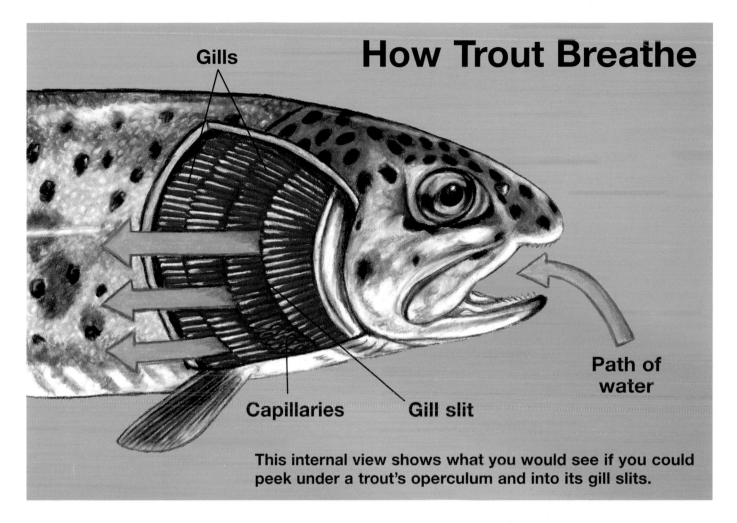

Gills

How Trout Breathe

Capillaries **Gill slit**

Path of water

This internal view shows what you would see if you could peek under a trout's operculum and into its gill slits.

Trout breathe through their **gills**. These organs draw oxygen out of the water in much the same way that humans' lungs draw oxygen from the air. Gills also expel poisonous carbon dioxide into the water, just as human lungs expel it into the air.

Gills are located in slits along the throat. The slits are protected by a bony flap called the **operculum** (oh-PUR-kyoo-luhm). To breathe, a trout first sucks water into its mouth. Then it opens its gill slits. Water flows through the mouth over the gills, where oxygen from the water enters tiny blood vessels called **capillaries**. At the same time, carbon dioxide passes from the capillaries into the water. The trout closes its mouth, pumping the water, with its load of carbon dioxide, out through the open slits. Then the process begins again.

The lateral line runs along the whole length of a trout's body. This rainbow trout's lateral line is easy to see because there is a rosy streak beside it.

The trout's sense organs, like those of other fish, are specialized for life underwater. A trout doesn't have ears on the outside of its head as a human does, but it can hear sounds with its inner ears. Trout also use an organ called the **lateral line** to sense the vibrations, or rapid movements, that travel through water.

The lateral line is made up of nerves that extend from the inner ears along both sides of the trout's body, just under the scales. The inner ears and lateral line help the trout detect other animals, such as an insect that the trout might eat, or a heron that might try to eat the trout.

To keep its balance, a trout relies on pebblelike structures called **otoliths** (OH-toh-liths), or ear stones. Located inside the inner ears, the otoliths help the trout detect which way is up, even in deep, dark water where the trout can't see. The otoliths press on tiny hairs that line the inner ear. When the fish is right side up, the otoliths rest at the bottom of the inner ear and press against the hairs there. If a big wave tosses the trout upside down, the otoliths strike the hairs at the top of the inner ear. The hairs signal the brain that the trout is upside down, and the trout will flip over.

Otoliths help biologists, too. Otoliths grow as a trout gets older. After a trout dies, its otoliths can be studied to tell how old it was. Biologists have found that most trout live 4 to 10 years. Lake trout in cold climates can live to be 65 years old or more.

The trout's other senses are also well suited to underwater life. Its powerful sense of smell lets it sniff its way through hundreds of miles of streams and never make a wrong turn. Although this seems remarkable to us, the trout's sense of smell is about average compared to other fish.

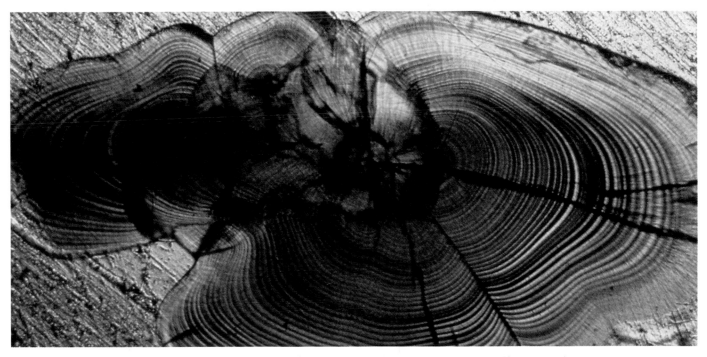

To determine the age of a fish that has died, biologists slice an otolith into thin sections (above) *and count the tiny rings.*

A trout's large, bulging eyes help it find food and avoid danger.

Trout rely on their their keen eyesight to find food. They can spot tiny insects drifting in the water several feet away. Because their eyes bulge out from their heads, trout can see above, below, and behind themselves, as well as straight ahead. If a tasty-looking insect passes behind a trout, the trout can see it, quickly turn around, and capture it. This ability also helps trout avoid being eaten by other animals. If a bigger fish or a heron tries to sneak up behind a trout, the trout can often spot the danger and dash to safety.

Trout that spend part of their lives in salt water require even more specialized features. They must adapt to a very different environment from the freshwater in which they grew up. Most fish that live in freshwater will die if they are put into salt water. Too much salt builds up in their tissues, and their organs stop working. But in trout that migrate to the ocean, the kidneys and gills can dispose of extra salt. This allows the trout to survive in the ocean. Most fish are adapted to live in either freshwater or salt water. Very few—including trout—are able to live in both habitats.

BUILT FOR SWIMMING

Trout are fast, graceful swimmers. They can spurt forward or change direction in an instant. They can also swim hundreds of miles in less than a month. Few other fish have this combination of speed and endurance.

Trout owe their swimming ability to several special features. Powerful muscles along each side of the fish bend its body from side to side. This whips the tail back and forth, driving the trout forward through the water.

Trout have powerful tails that propel them through the water quickly.

In addition to strong muscles, trout have seven **fins** that help them swim. The caudal (CAW-duhl) fin, located at the end of the tail, helps push the trout through the water and acts as a rudder to turn the trout left or right. The large dorsal fin on the trout's back, and the small anal fin on its belly near the tail, keep the trout from rolling over in the water.

On the trout's belly, two pectoral fins act as brakes when the trout needs to stop in a hurry. Behind the pectoral fins, two pelvic fins help the trout move quickly upward through the water. The pectoral and pelvic fins also help the trout steer smoothly and accurately.

Trout have an eighth fin, the adipose (AD-uh-pose) fin. Located just behind the dorsal fin, the adipose fin is a storage place for fat. It isn't much help in swimming.

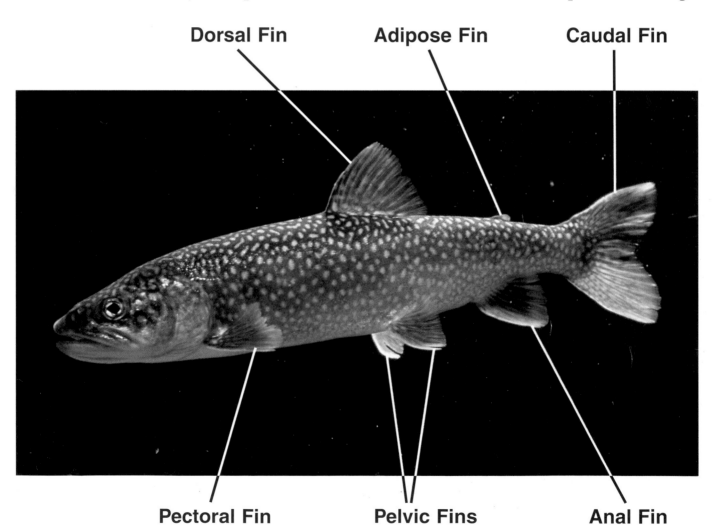

Dorsal Fin **Adipose Fin** **Caudal Fin**

Pectoral Fin **Pelvic Fins** **Anal Fin**

Thanks to its swim bladder, a trout can hover near the surface (above) *or sink deep into the water* (below).

An organ called the **swim bladder** helps the trout control the depth at which it hovers in the water. For example, if the trout finds food or a safe place to rest at 20 feet (6.1 m) underwater, it can use its swim bladder to easily stay at that depth.

The swim bladder is a long, sack-shaped organ connected to the throat by a narrow tube. It lies just below the spine. When a trout is very young, its swim bladder is empty. Since the young trout is heavier than water, it sinks unless it swims upward. So the trout swims to the surface of the water and gulps air into its swim bladder, which swells up like a skinny balloon. This makes the trout lighter than the water around it. Then the trout can float, as if it had a life preserver inside it.

Throughout its life, the trout can burp out some air so it can sink deeper into the water. It can also shut the tube to hold the air in and keep from sinking. A trout can add more air to its swim bladder at any time by swimming to the surface and taking another gulp. It can also fill or empty the bladder by exchanging oxygen and other gases through capillaries that surround the swim bladder.

19

FINDING A MEAL

Trout are **predators**, which means they hunt and eat other animals, called **prey**. The kind of prey a trout eats and its method of hunting depend on how big the trout is and where it lives. In general, the larger the trout, the larger the prey it eats.

Trout that eat large prey use the rows of needle-sharp teeth that line their jaws and part of the roof of the mouth. All these teeth help trout capture and hold onto their prey. Trout don't usually chew their food. Instead, they swallow it in chunks. In the trout's stomach, the food is broken down into smaller pieces and digested.

Trout teeth are covered with a hard, glossy coating called enamel, just as human teeth are. If a trout's tooth falls out or breaks off, a new one grows to take its place.

Trout that live in the ocean eat large prey such as fish and squid. Ocean-dwelling trout may cruise far away from land or stay near the shoreline, depending on where they find food. Although each trout travels and hunts on its own, an area with a rich food supply may attract many trout at one time.

Many trout that live in lakes eat fish, but some don't. Instead, some trout eat insects and a lot of **zooplankton** (ZOH-oh-PLANK-tuhn), microscopic animals that live in water. Trout catch huge numbers of these tiny prey by swimming along with their mouths open. In the trout's throat, near the gills, are comb-like structures called **gill rakers**. When water flows over the gills, zooplankton get caught on the gill rakers. Then the trout swallows a nutritious mouthful.

A cutthroat trout cruises, holding its mouth open to catch a meal of zooplankton.

Trout that live in streams eat some fish and zooplankton but rely on insects for most of their food. Trout in streams don't just swim around looking for food. Instead, each trout lurks in a spot called a **lie**, where it faces into the current and watches for insects or other bits of food to drift by. Whenever the trout sees something that might be food, it swims toward the object to get a better look and to smell it.

If the trout decides the object drifting by doesn't look or smell like food, it returns to its lie. But if the object seems to be food, the trout darts forward, whips open its mouth, and sucks in the morsel. The trout swallows the prey whole, then returns to its lie to watch for more prey. It remembers how its meal looked, smelled, and tasted, so it will be ready the next time a similar object drifts by.

Sometimes a trout gets fooled. It snaps up a tiny stick or bit of leaf. When this happens, the trout spits out the object and goes back to its lie to try again. As before, it remembers the experience. It will try not to be fooled the next time.

A brown trout waits in its lie, hoping to nab a tasty snack. A good lie has crannies, made by logs or rocks, where the fish can hide if it senses danger.

A trout's-eye view of a drifting mayfly

Where do trout find insects to eat? Insects that live on land, such as ants, crickets, and grasshoppers, sometimes fall into the water. In late summer, hundreds of grasshoppers may end up in a single stream each day. They can't swim or get back into the air, so they float helplessly on the surface, where they are easily snapped up by trout lurking below.

Other insects, including some types of flies, live in the stream for part of their lives. The adults lay their eggs in the water. The young, called nymphs, that hatch from these eggs stay near the bottom of the stream for weeks or months as they grow toward adulthood. The stream's current sometimes carries them out of their hiding places. Then a hungry trout may see the nymphs and gobble them up.

These insects also fall prey to trout when they become adults and travel up through the water to the surface. Millions of flies may emerge from one part of a stream within an hour. Trout feast on the swimming insects. Sometimes a trout is so eager to nab a tasty fly that it jumps all the way out of the water.

ON THE MOVE

Trout that live their whole lives in small streams may grow up, breed, and die within just a few hundred feet of where they were born. But most trout migrate from one place to another at different times in their lives, as their needs change. They may migrate to warmer areas in winter or to cooler areas in summer. Often they migrate to find better sources of food.

Almost all trout migrate to their birthplaces to **spawn,** or produce young. The places where adult trout live are usually not good places for baby trout to grow up. The water is either too deep or too fast, or it has too many predators that might eat the baby trout, or it doesn't have the right kind of food for young trout to eat. So trout return to safer waters when it's time to spawn.

An adult bull trout (Salvelinus confluentus) *can easily make its home in a fast, bubbling stream, but young trout need to grow up in slow water.*

Brook trout swim through a Wyoming stream on their way to spawn.

This is when the trout's keen sense of smell works its magic. Trout find their way back to their birthplaces mainly by smell. They remember the scent of their home stream and of all the other streams they must follow to get there.

How far a trout migrates depends on where it lives. Trout that live their whole lives in a single stream move only a short distance to spawn. Trout that live in a big river may migrate upstream until they reach a smaller stream that flows into the river.

Most trout that live in lakes migrate into streams when it is time to spawn. After spawning, they migrate back to the lake. In lakes that do not have streams flowing into or out of them, the trout spawn in the lake itself. Even then, they usually migrate to a part of the lake that is safer for baby trout than the part where the adults live.

Trout that live in the ocean when they are adults make the longest and most difficult migration of all. The ocean provides a rich diet that helps trout grow large and strong. But baby trout need freshwater. Their kidneys and gills aren't yet adapted for life in salt water. So adults that live in the ocean must migrate into freshwater to spawn. After spawning, the adults return to their feeding areas in the ocean. When their young grow large enough to make the trip—6 to 10 inches long (15-25 cm)—they will migrate to the ocean as their parents did.

Trout that migrate between the ocean and freshwater are called **sea-run** trout. In some places, their spawning migration is famous because of the huge number of trout that move up the river, displaying their vivid spawning colors. Nearly a million trout may crowd into a single river, their flashing red bellies and cheeks making a spectacular show.

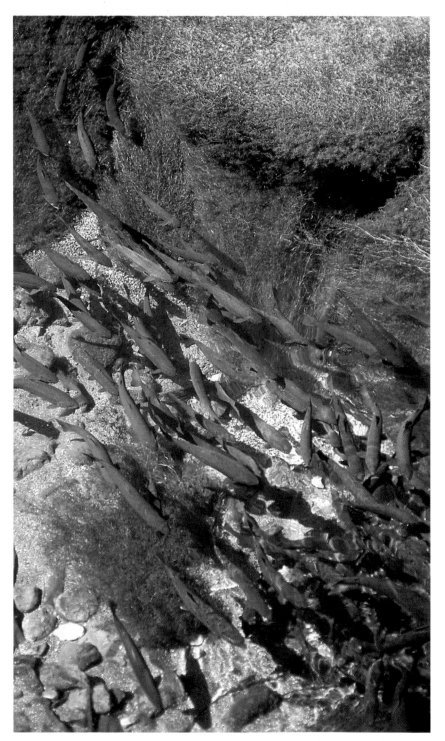

Migrating rainbow trout fill a stream with waving tails and streaks of pink.

A migrating steelhead makes a stunning leap over a waterfall.

Although the trout's migration looks beautiful to humans, for the trout it is a difficult time. They may have to swim hundreds of miles through the ocean just to reach the river that leads to their spawning area. Once they enter the river, they still have a long way to go. They swim through many different habitats as they travel past cities, farms, and forests. When they encounter small waterfalls, they must jump through the air to reach the stream at the top of the falls.

An otter (left) makes a meal out of a trout, while an egret (below) fishes for its supper. Predators are only one of the many challenges migrating trout face.

Migrating trout face many threats. Predators such as bears and eagles scoop up and eat many of the trout, which are often so crowded in the river that they can't hide or escape. Despite these dangers, in years past most trout survived and completed their journey.

In recent decades, human activities have made migration even more difficult. Pollution can keep trout from reaching their spawning grounds because it covers up the normal smells in the water. When that happens, the trout are not able to find their home spawning area. They may spawn elsewhere, sometimes in an area that is not good for young trout. Or they may not spawn at all.

Dams, which are built across rivers to provide electricity and store water for people, can block trout on their way to their spawning areas. If the trout can't reach their home stream, they may not spawn. If they don't spawn for several years in a row, that group of trout will die out. To help adult trout complete their migration, some dams now include fish ladders. These steplike structures allow the trout to jump up the dam about a foot at a time.

The Savage Rapids Dam (below) in Oregon has a fish ladder (right) that helps trout and other fish make their way up the river.

SPAWNING

A female trout that survives the migration to her spawning area must then choose a good place to lay her eggs. This place is called her **redd**. The size of the redd depends on the size of the female trout. A small female may lay fewer than 100 eggs and need just 1 square foot (0.1 sq m) for her redd. A large female may lay up to 12,000 eggs and need over 100 square feet (9.3 sq m). Most trout females lay between 1,000 and 5,000 eggs.

The redd must provide a safe place for **embryos**, or developing babies, to grow. So the female seeks a redd where the gravel is clean and free of mud or sand, which could smother the baby trout.

The gravel must be just the right size to let the embryos slip down into spaces between the rocks, where they can safely grow and develop.

When the female finds a good place for her redd, she starts to dig an **egg pocket**. She lies on her side on the gravel and thrashes her tail. This sweeps the gravel aside so that a shallow hole forms. As the female does this, several males approach her. The largest male usually chases smaller males away. He nips at them with the **kype,** or hook, that developed on his lower jaw just before spawning season. He will be the one to mate with the female.

This male tiger trout, a cross between a brook trout and a brown trout, is ready to spawn. He nips at a rival with his kype.

Above: *A pair of brook trout have found a safe place to spawn.*
Right: *After the trout have spawned, tiny embryos drop into the egg pocket.*

When the egg pocket is deep enough, mating begins. The female hovers just above the egg pocket. She shivers and arches her back. The male swims up beside her and arches his back. They open their mouths very wide. From an opening near her tail, the female releases tiny, round eggs. At the same time, the male releases **milt**, a milky fluid containing millions of sperm. Eggs and sperm mix in the egg pocket. When an egg and a sperm join, an embryo forms. The embryos drop into spaces in the gravel.

After mating, the female moves to one side of the egg pocket and starts to dig another one. As she digs, the gravel she moves covers the first egg pocket. This helps protect the embryos there.

The male swims away. Both he and the female will mate many times over the next several days or weeks, but not always with each other.

Spawning takes a lot of energy, and most trout don't eat much during their migration or while in the spawning area. When they finish spawning, they are weak and hungry. The trout leave the spawning area a few at a time and drift downstream. As the current carries them, they start to eat again. Slowly, they become stronger.

Like the upstream migration, this trip is very dangerous. Dams again pose a serious threat to the trout. Many dams contain turbine engines that spin like giant pinwheels as water flows through them. As the trout swim downstream, they may be sucked into these turbines and chopped into little pieces. Many make it through safely, but thousands of trout die in turbines every year. In the Pacific Northwest, many rivers that once were home to hundreds of thousands of trout now have none.

Trout that survive their downstream migration eventually reach the feeding area in the stream, lake, or ocean from which they came. They stay there for a year or two. Then they migrate back upstream to spawn again.

Barges can help trout pass dams on the way downstream. The fish are trapped in tanks near the dam, then loaded onto the barge. After the barge passes the dam, the fish are released. Scientists are trying to find out whether barging is an effective way to help trout survive.

GROWING UP

Back in the egg pockets, the embryos left behind by the adult trout start to develop into tiny fish. For the first few days, they are very fragile. Any rough treatment, such as a sudden rush of fast water, will kill them. As they get older, the embryos become stronger.

How fast they develop depends on the time of year their parents spawned. The embryos of trout that spawn in fall take up to 9 months to develop, because the cold temperatures of fall and winter slow their growth. The embryos of trout that spawn in spring develop much more quickly. In both cases, the embryos finish their development in late spring or early summer.

During this time, the embryos get nourishment from **yolk** stored in each egg. Yolk contains proteins, carbohydrates, and fats to help the embryos grow.

When the embryos have developed into baby trout, they hatch out of their eggs. They thrash back and forth, tearing the thin, delicate shells that enclose them. The trout are only about 0.6 inches long (1.5 cm).

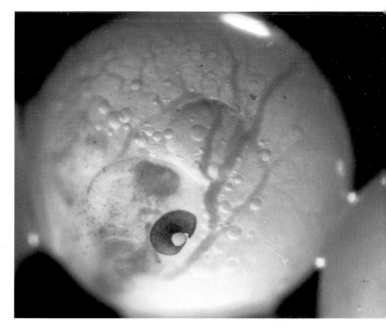

Above: *Inside the embryo, two large, dark eyes form, as well as organs such as the heart, stomach, and swim bladder.*
Below: *Hatching time. The trout on the left and in the back are shaking themselves free from their eggs. The trout in front, on the right, has already emerged from its egg.*

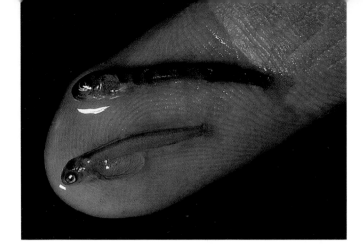

Left: *A fry (above) fits easily on a human finger but is still larger than the newly hatched trout below it.*

A large ball of yolk continues to nourish each young trout but also makes swimming very hard. The young trout stay down in the gravel until they have used up almost all of the yolk. Then they are called **fry**. They are about 1.1 inches long (2.8 cm).

Fry can swim well enough to wiggle up through gaps in the gravel and reach the open water of the stream. Soon after leaving the gravel, the fry swim to the surface to gulp air into their swim bladders. Then they stay in shallow areas or near the sides of the stream, where the current is not too strong.

Fry must learn what to eat and how to capture it. Fry usually eat tiny insects, but it takes the fry a while to learn what is good and not so good to eat. At first, fry try to eat anything they can catch. They learn by tasting many things. They spit out things that taste bad and learn to recognize what will taste good.

Above: *These rainbow trout are just 2 days old. Each trout gets food from the ball of yolk under its belly.*

Above: *By the age of 3 months, these rainbow trout fry have grown to about 1 inch (2.5 cm). They are learning how to find food and avoid predators.*

34

This is a very dangerous time for the fry. Some don't find enough to eat. Some get swept away by the current. Some are eaten by predators or killed by diseases. About 95 of every 100 fry will die. If a large female trout lays 12,000 eggs, no more than 600 of the fry that develop from them will survive to become **parr**. At this stage they are a few inches (several centimeters) long. They are silver with dark oval patches called parr marks on their sides.

Although a parr swims well and is able to catch fast prey, it is still not big enough to have a lie of its own. Instead, it roams around the stream in search of food. While parr hunt, they may also be hunted by other fish or by fish-eating birds. Parr must learn to stay away from larger trout that might eat them and to hide behind rocks and logs whenever they can.

Parr must grow a lot before they are large enough to migrate to the lake, sea, or large stream where they will live as adults. In areas where summers are short and there is little to eat, the parr stage lasts 3 or 4 years. In warmer areas, with long summers and abundant food, it lasts just a few months.

This rainbow trout parr is about a year old and 5 inches long (12.5 cm).

When the young trout are ready to migrate to the adult feeding area, they are called **juveniles** (JOO-veh-niles). Their parr marks fade, and adult colors and patterns appear. Over the next several weeks, the juveniles swim downstream to the feeding area, where they will grow into adults.

Juvenile sea-run trout on their way to the ocean are called **smolts**. Their parr marks fade, but instead of taking on the vivid colors of freshwater trout, smolts remain silver all over. Their bodies become more slender. Their kidneys and gills change to allow the smolts to live in salt water. Soon after these changes take place, the smolts gather into large groups and migrate to the ocean. Millions of smolts may migrate down a single river. Like their parents before them, smolts face danger from predators, pollution, and dams.

The smolts that survive their journey to the ocean find rich food that enables them to grow much more quickly than juveniles that stay in freshwater. Juvenile rainbow trout weigh about a quarter of a pound (114 g) when they migrate to the adult feeding areas. Those that become steelheads and go to sea grow so fast there that they weigh 8 to 12 pounds (3.6-5.4 kg) within 2 years. But freshwater trout need 4 years to grow to just 4.4 pounds (2.0 kg). Most never reach the size of their sea-run relatives.

Still, because lake-dwelling trout can live many years longer than sea-run trout, those that survive grow to be the biggest trout of all. Some reach almost a yard long and weigh nearly 50 pounds (22.7 kg). Trout that live their whole lives in small mountain streams may never grow more than 5 inches long (12.5 cm) or weigh more than a few ounces (about 100 g).

Both freshwater and sea-run trout stay in their feeding areas for a few years of eating and growing before they are ready to spawn. Then, guided by their sense of smell, they head back up the same stream they migrated down as juveniles. As before, many of the migrating trout do not survive the journey. Of all the hundreds or thousands of eggs that a single female lays throughout her life, an average of only two mature trout will return to their home stream and spawn to create a new generation.

Adult trout can be as small as a human hand (above) *or much larger. This bull trout* (left) *is 30 inches long (75 cm).*

TROUT IN DANGER

Trout face many dangers during their lives. Floods, dry spells, ice, diseases, and predators all take their toll. Over time, trout have developed ways to cope with these natural dangers. Mucus, for example, protects trout from infection and helps them swim away from predators quickly.

Recently trout have faced new dangers that come from human uses of the land and water. We change trout habitats in many ways. We pollute water with insecticides and with chemicals from mines, factories, and cars. This pollution can kill trout or their prey. When we cut down the trees near a stream, or let too many cattle graze along its banks, soil washes into the water. The soil can kill the insects trout need to eat. It can also kill embryos and fry by making it hard for them to get enough oxygen. Cutting down trees also hurts trout because it removes shade. Then the water gets too warm for trout to survive. Even water that is 80°F (27°C)—much cooler than your bathwater—will kill most trout.

Trout have always had to cope with natural disasters such as dry spells (top) *and floods* (left).

Right: *Loggers have left a border of trees along this shore to shade the lake and prevent soil from washing away.*
Bottom: *Water pollution has killed these fish.*
Bottom right: *Cows have eaten all the plants and trampled the earth along the banks of this river, causing soil to wash into the water.*

Activities like these have damaged the habitat of Gila trout *(Oncorhynchus gilae gilae)*, which live in small streams in New Mexico and Arizona. Gila trout have become **endangered**—all members of the species may soon die. Biologists are working to help the Gila trout survive. These efforts are important because every species makes a unique contribution to its environment. For example, if Gila trout disappear, the animals that usually eat them would have less food and might also die. Even the wastes—urine and feces—produced by Gila trout might be needed by other animals and plants in the stream.

Overfishing, or catching too many trout, causes problems in some areas. Most states try to prevent this by limiting the number and size of fish that can be caught. Many people practice "catch and release" fishing. A fisher who catches a trout gently removes the fishhook and lets the trout go back into the water. This allows fishers to enjoy their hobby without killing the fish.

Above: *A fisherman releases a brown trout, unharmed, back into its stream.*
Left: *This Gila trout is one of the few remaining of its kind.*

Above: *This rainbow trout's body shows the deadly effects of whirling disease.*
Left: *Stocking trout into this Arizona river could be both helpful and harmful.*

Stocking, or putting fish that were raised in captivity into streams and lakes, also affects trout. This is how the trout's range expanded to places like southern Africa. Stocking provides more trout for people to catch, and it gives the stocked trout a chance to survive in the wild.

But stocking creates many problems, because adding a new species to a habitat affects the animals and plants that already live there. When trout are stocked in places where other trout live, the stocked trout compete with the native trout for food and for hiding places. They also breed with native trout, so the pure line of wild trout can be lost. Gila trout faced this problem when rainbow trout were stocked into streams where the Gila trout lived.

Stocked trout often carry diseases that attack the wild trout. One of these, called whirling disease, was brought to American rivers by stocked European rainbow trout in the 1950s. The disease makes a young trout's spine curve. When the trout tries to swim, it goes in a circle—it whirls. These fish have a very hard time catching prey, and most of them die young. Biologists are trying to find ways to cure whirling disease and prevent its spread. So far, there is no cure for it.

Yellowstone Lake, home of the Yellowstone cutthroat trout

Sometimes trout get into new areas by human mischief. In 1994, lake trout were discovered in Yellowstone Lake, the largest lake in Yellowstone National Park. They had never lived there before, but their size suggested that they had been in the lake since the 1960s. Yellowstone Park biologists think someone put them there as a prank.

The lake trout are threatening their cousins, the Yellowstone cutthroat trout (*Oncorhynchus clarki bouvieri*) that have lived in the lake for thousands of years. Lake trout grow faster and larger than Yellowstone cutthroats do. They eat Yellowstone cutthroats and chase them away from the best feeding areas.

Biologists are trying to figure out how to kill the lake trout without harming the lake's other inhabitants. If the lake trout cannot be controlled, the Yellowstone cutthroats will die out. That would be bad for the lake and for the creatures that live in and near it. Yellowstone cutthroats contribute to the ecology of the lake in ways that lake trout do not. Yellowstone cutthroats provide food for grizzly bears, bald eagles, otters, and other predators when the cutthroats migrate from the lake into streams to spawn. Lake trout don't migrate into streams. Instead, they spawn in the lake, where predators can't reach them. Without the cutthroats as a source of food, those predators could go hungry.

Yellowstone Lake's cutthroat trout may vanish forever if they are not protected.

Although the dangers people pose to trout will be hard to overcome, we have a responsibility to protect these amazing fish. The many species of trout provide us with food, sport, and a glimpse of life underwater. But trout deserve to survive for their own sake and for the sake of the creatures that share their habitats. Fortunately, people are beginning to understand how the things we do can help or harm trout. As we learn more, we can better protect these beautiful fish and their wild homes.

GLOSSARY

adaptations: changes that enable a plant or animal to survive in an environment

capillaries: tiny blood vessels in which gases are exchanged

egg pocket: a shallow hole dug in gravel by a female to hold baby trout

embryo: an animal in the early stages of development, before birth or hatching

endangered: at risk of losing all members of a type of plant or animal forever

fins: flaps that extend from the body of a fish and help it to swim and store fat

fry: young trout that have just left the gravel of the stream bottom. They are no longer nourished by yolk and begin to hunt for food.

gill rakers: fingerlike structures in a trout's throat that snag microscopic animals for the trout to eat

gills: organs used by fish to breathe underwater

habitat: the kind of environment in which a plant or animal lives. A habitat includes the kinds of animals and plants that live in it, the type of soil and water it has, and its climate.

hormones: chemicals in the body that cause specific changes, such as the bright colors of trout during mating season

juveniles: young trout that migrate to the adult feeding area

kype: a hook that forms at the tip of the lower jaw of a male trout during mating season

lateral line: an organ along the trout's sides that senses vibrations in the water

lie: a spot in a stream where a trout waits and watches for prey

migrate: to move to a new area for a specific purpose, such as feeding or mating

milt: a milky fluid that contains sperm and is released by male trout during mating

mucus: a slimy substance on the surface of a fish that helps it move quickly in the water and protects against infections

operculum: bony flap that covers the gills

otoliths: ear stones that help a trout maintain its balance in the water. Otoliths can be measured to determine a trout's age.

parr: young trout that swim and hunt well and have dark oval marks on their sides

predators: animals that hunt other animals

prey: animals that are eaten by other animals

range: the geographic area in which a plant or animal lives

redd: an area on the bottom of a stream or lake where eggs are laid

scales: clear oval disks in the skin that protect a trout from injury and infection

sea-run: trout that live in the ocean as adults and return to freshwater to mate

smolts: young trout that travel from streams to adult feeding areas in the ocean

spawn: to mate, or produce young

species: a kind of animal or plant

stocking: putting trout that were raised in captivity into lakes and streams

swim bladder: an organ that holds air like a balloon and helps a fish stay at a certain depth in the water

yolk: nutrients stored in eggs to nourish baby trout as they develop

zooplankton: microscopic animals that live in water

INDEX

ABOUT THE AUTHOR

Richard Alan Hannon

Cherie Winner has loved spending time outdoors since her youth in southern Michigan, where she fished for bluegills. It wasn't until years later that she became fascinated with trout. Since the 1980s she has fished for (and sometimes even caught!) rainbow, brook, brown, and cutthroat trout. Dr. Winner's fishing travels have taken her to alpine lakes, beaver ponds, small creeks, and large rivers throughout the Rocky Mountain region, especially in the Yellowstone area. She moved to Wyoming in 1991, but only partly to be closer to trout. Dr. Winner is the author of the Carolrhoda Nature Watch books *Salamanders*, *Coyotes*, and *The Sunflower Family*.